STEPHEN POLLAN'S
FOOLPROOF GUIDE

TO RENOVATING
YOUR KITCHEN

STEPHEN M. POLLAN
& MARK LEVINE
ILLUSTRATIONS BY BETSY BAYTOS

A FIRESIDE BOOK
PUBLISHED BY SIMON & SCHUSTER

FIRESIDE
Rockefeller Center
1230 Avenue of the Americas
New York, NY 10020

FIRESIDE and colophon are registered trademarks
of Simon & Schuster Inc.

Designed by Irving Perkins Associates

Manufactured in the United States of America

1   3   5   7   9   10   8   6   4   2

Library of Congress Cataloging-in-Publication Data

Pollan, Stephen M.
Stephen Pollan's foolproof guide to renovating your kitchen /
Stephen M. Pollan & Mark Levine: illustrations by Betsy Baytos.
p.   cm.
1. Kitchens—Remodeling   2. Contractors—Selection and
appointment   I. Levine, Mark, date.   II. Title.
TH4816.3.K58P65   1997
643'. 3–dc21   96-48907
                                                      CIP
ISBN 978-0-6848-0227-5

CONTENTS

INTRODUCTION

I'm probably the only person writing about home renovations who's against "doing it yourself." For most of us, our home is the single largest asset we have. It, or at least the equity we have in it, can help fund our retirement, the education of children, or provide seed money for a business of our own. Therefore we should be very conservative with our homes.

An amateurish renovation can detract dramatically from the value of a home and make it much more difficult to sell. Don't rationalize your doing it yourself by saying you'll never sell your home. Every home, including yours, is eventually sold. If you don't sell it, your survivors will.

And take it from someone who has written ten how-to books: no book can replace the expertise and experience of a good professional or a skilled tradesperson.

Americans have an almost innate urge

to be self-reliant. That's probably because we're a nation of immigrants who carved a society out of the wilderness. The urge for self-reliance probably accounts for our becoming a nation of entrepreneurs and inventors, a beacon of democracy, and the wealthiest and most powerful country in the world.

But there's also a dark side to self-reliance. We've somehow internalized the notion that delegating authority to others, or hiring others to do things for us is a sign of weakness; it's almost un-American.

Nowhere is the foolishness of this attitude more apparent than in home renova-

tions. Most people, regardless of whether or not they know the difference between a circular saw and a saber saw, think they're able either to do construction work on their own, or at the very least manage a construction job. Nearly every person who has hung a shelf thinks he or she can build a deck.

Our lack of respect for people who work with their hands contributes to this misconception. We fail to realize just as much learning goes into becoming a good carpenter or a general contractor as a lawyer.

Our childhoods also contribute to the misconception—we progress from blocks to Legos; we build sand castles at the beach with toy tools and miniature bull-dozers. Our growing national interest in cooking and dining feed it as well, as do all the home improvement shows on televi-sion and the retailers who make millions selling paint and nails and lumber to do-it-yourselfers.

A man who grew up playing with Legos, spends Saturday afternoons watching *This Old House*, and who has successfully hung shelves in the den wants to remodel his own kitchen. A woman who grew up playing with a Suzy Homemaker Oven, reads *Gourmet* religiously, and runs her own business wants to plan and manage her own kitchen renovation project.

It's admirable to want to do these things yourself, but it's a huge mistake to do it. There's nothing wrong with indulging the urge to tinker or build. And if you think you'll get pleasure or satisfaction from planning managing a renovation job, that's wonderful. Just make sure you're supervising the renovation of a dollhouse or a doghouse, not your own house. That way, if you mess up, the only one to suffer will be Barbie or Rover.

You should be concentrating your efforts on the overall administration of your kitchen renovation project. That doesn't mean surrendering control to either a design professional or a general contractor. It means functioning as the chief executive officer of the project: overseeing the planning, making the policy decisions, delegating the authority to implement those decisions, making sure the project stays on course, and paying the bills.

You shouldn't be worrying about whether you need a carbide-tip drill bit or if the electrician should be called in before the plumber. Instead, you should be concerned with:

- getting your goals and timing down
- finding and choosing someone to draw your plans
- contracting and collaborating with your planner
- finding and checking up on candidate contractors
- analyzing bids and choosing your general contractor
- contracting with your contractor
- making the dollar decisions
- dealing with problems during and after the job

That should be more than enough to satisfy even the most rugged individualist. I know it's been more than enough to satisfy me. And I've gone through three major and a couple of minor kitchen renovations of my own. In addition, I've coached my clients through more than a hundred kitchen renovations in the past thirty years.

Finally, a few notes of thanks. While I've had a great deal of experience serving as the CEO of many kitchen renovations, I was lucky enough to also be able to draw on the more specific expertise of many skilled craftspersons, prudent professionals, and savvy designers. I'd particularly like to thank Erwin Shustak, Esq., for his sage advice, and Charles Mount and Florence Perchuk for their creative suggestions. Last, but certainly not least, Mark Levine and I would like to thank Gabrielle Kleinman for her tireless and unstinting efforts with the manuscript.

—*Stephen M. Pollan*

How to Use This Book

This book is designed to be used, not just read. The project of renovating your kitchen has been broken down into a series of seven stages. Each of these stages has then been broken down into an easy-to-follow series of steps. Tips and warnings about each step are also provided. Before acting on any individual step, read through the book, including all the tips and warnings, once. Then, go back to the beginning and proceed through the process, using the book as a guide. When you complete a step, check the box labeled "Done," and move on to the next step. Avoid the temptation to jump ahead or do things out of order. The stages and steps have been designed to build on one another and have been written based on my more than thirty years' experience of going through this exact process.

—Stephen M. Pollan

GETTING YOUR GOALS AND TIMING DOWN

Believe me, this is no ordinary renovation project you're about to embark on. Kitchen renovations are simultaneously the most complex and the most psychologically charged home improvement projects. They can lead to both financial and emotional disaster. That's why it's essential to begin with a very firm foundation by getting your goals and timing down.

1 **Focus on the emotional and psychological baggage attached to a kitchen renovation.** The kitchen is the most important room in the house—it is the hearth of the home. The kitchen is not simply the room where you eat and cook, it is the place where the family gathers and is the center of family life. This is the room where the interests and tastes of all family members intersect. The kids' artwork decorates the refrigerator, the mail and newspapers inevitably end up strewn on a counter, and even dinner guests congregate for predinner wine as the cooks/hosts finish their task. So when you begin this project, ask yourself: Will the improvement increase your family's pleasure in your home? Will it enhance your quality of life?

☐ **Done**

Tip 1.1: Before you start, consult with all family members. What are their individual needs? Since everyone uses the room, everyone should have a say. Open communication at the beginning will save fights and disappointments down the road.

Tip 1.2: Buy a variety of home and architecture magazines and call kitchen showrooms for their catalogs. These are tremendous sources of ideas, and looking at pictures will help you figure out what you do and don't like.

Tip 1.3: Don't be afraid to reach for the sky when you're brainstorming. Today, much of what you see in the upscale publications can be duplicated at knock-off prices.

Tip 1.4: Make a pro and con list—what do you love about your existing kitchen and what do you hate? Then jot down how you would like to change those "hates" into "loves."

Tip 1.5: Sketch out your own set of plans. You don't need to be Frank Lloyd Wright to draw a rough resemblance of a kitchen floor plan. The drawing is mostly simple lines and shapes, which are used to represent walls, appliances, cabinets, etc. Look at the kitchen layouts in planning books to see how they're done, or check out what computer programs are available. All you're trying to do is get your ideas down on paper so you'll have an easier time conveying them to the planner.

Warning 1.6: What makes a kitchen renovation so difficult is that it leads to spousal polarization. My wife and I had the biggest fights of our forty-year marriage over this issue. It came down to her desire for top-of-the-line everything versus my budget worries. Inevitably, one spouse will get caught up in the design, planning, and quality issues, leaving the other the job of controlling the purse strings. This is a recipe for disaster unless you consciously work against it.

Tip 1.7: Think about how long you plan to stay in your house. If you plan to stay for the long term, your emotional and quality-of-life considerations should play the more significant role in the kitchen renovation process. If you're only there for the short term, your financial concerns should drive the project.

2 Determine what kind of kitchen renovation will best achieve a balance between your emotional and financial needs. Now that all family members have given input as to what they want, you have to figure out how extensive a kitchen renovation you can afford. Generally, renovations fall into four categories. *Face-lifts* involve installing new appliances and light fixtures, repainting walls and ceilings, refinishing or refacing cabinets, and having new flooring installed. *System upgrades* are improvements to the functional quality of the kitchen, such as replacing windows and doors or improving the electrical, plumbing, heating, or cooling systems. *Space additions* are those renovations that add to the actual living space of the home. *Remodeling* involves anything that alters the floor plan of your kitchen.

☐ **Done**

Tip 2.1: When you want to add character to an otherwise generic kitchen, or simply spruce up and replace an outdated, worn look, a face-lift is generally the most inexpensive type of renovation.

Tip 2.2: While system upgrades are not very glamorous or exciting, they can add immeasurably to your comfort and happiness. They also make your home more energy efficient and may pay for themselves by the time you sell.

Warning 2.3: Upgrades often require getting behind walls and replacing piping, wiring, and ventilation ducts, which can be costly.

Tip 2.4: For less than the cost of buying a new home, a structural addition gives you the space you crave.

Tip 2.5: Remodeling is an alternative to a space addition. It allows you to create space within the existing structure of your kitchen for less money.

Tip 2.6: Whatever project you choose, try to contain the scope at the start, because there is a tendency for the project to take on a life of its own once it's under way. The process becomes organic and all the participants (you, the architect or designer, the contractor) are easily seduced. Everyone tends to lose sight of the cost and lets the kitchen grow beyond all the carefully laid plans.

3 **Acknowledge that there's a second financial consideration: how your renovation will affect the value of your home.** Kitchen renovations have the potential to add to the value of your home. But no matter what kind of renovation you do, your home's value will never climb above a certain point. In general, kitchen renovations make sense in five situations: when you want more space, but can't afford to buy another home; when you want to make your kitchen more functional; when you want to increase the pleasure you get from your kitchen; when you want to add character to an otherwise generic kitchen; and when you're seeking to boost the value of your home.

☐ **Done**

Tip 3.1: Kitchen renovations make the most financial sense when they bring a home from the low end of the range to the high end in your local geographic area. If you're not sure about local market values and what the effect might be of the renovation you're planning, consult a real estate broker or appraiser. You shouldn't spend more than roughly 10–20 percent of your home's current value—don't over-improve!

Warning 3.2: Luxury add-ons, such as restaurant appli-ances, skylights, and fireplaces, are extremely costly. And they won't add signif-icantly to your home because they are unique to taste. If homes in your area sell for from $100,000 to $130,000, even your deluxe, restau-rant-quality kitchen won't get you more than $130,000.

Tip 3.3: The cost of a face-lift can be almost entirely recouped if you stick with neutral colors and mid-range appliances.

Warning 3.4: Kitchen face-lifts decrease in value over time as appliances become outmoded and finishes begin to lose their sparkle.

Warning 3.5: The cost of upgrading a system can be recouped only while the system is young. Still, adequate and aging is better than inadequate and aging.

Tip 3.6: A well-done space addition that fits or augments a home's appearance and reflects the needs and wants of most buyers can add to your home's value.

Warning 3.7: Make sure the addition doesn't destroy the internal or external appearance or character of your home. An out-of-character addition can actually decrease your home's value.

Warning 3.8: Though you may want to remodel to create an eating area, keep in mind that it is a more complex and costly renovation than a face-lift. However, a remodeling project can be a great investment if it makes your home more like others in the area.

Warning 3.9: A poorly thought out and executed remodeling job—one that destroys the flow and/or character of a home—can actually reduce your home's value. A good remodeling job will be invisible. People should be able to walk through your house and not realize the kitchen has been remodeled.

4 **Give some thought to the timing of your project before jumping into it.** Realize that a kitchen is the most complicated room in the house. To renovate it takes more time than doing any other room because every trade is involved from plumbers to electricians to carpenters, and the work must be coordinated so that elements of the project are completed in the appropriate sequence. It makes a seemingly small job enormous in reality.

☐ **Done**

Tip 4.1: An architect, designer, or kitchen planner will set your ideas down on paper. It takes about four to six weeks to find your architect or planner, and about a month for them to complete a set of plans.

Tip 4.5: Because of good weather conditions, GCs and subs are busiest from April through September doing work that requires being outdoors. By scheduling your project for January, February, or March, you'll be able to take advantage of their eagerness for indoor work during off months. Not only are prices likely to drop, but the likelihood of your having the contractor's undivided attention during this period is stronger. For those who live in the North, don't be concerned if your job includes some external work. Arrange with the GC to seal off the work site from the rest of the house.

Tip 4.5: Because of good weather conditions, GCs and subs are busiest from April through September doing work that requires being outdoors. By scheduling your project for January, February, or March, you'll be able to take advantage of their eagerness for indoor work during off months. Not only are prices likely to drop, but the likelihood of your having the contractor's undivided attention during this period is stronger. For those who live in the North, don't be concerned if your job includes some external work. Arrange with the GC to seal off the work site from the rest of the house.

Tip 4.6: Generally speaking, a face-lift needs about nine months' lead time. So if the target completion date is September 15, start January 15. A system upgrade needs about seven months' lead time and a space addition or remodeling project needs about eleven months.

Tip 4.7: Don't become anxious if your renovation schedule doesn't go like clockwork. Sometimes it takes longer than you expect to come up with plans or to find and interview GCs. Be flexible, because the schedule (within a couple of weeks) is less important than getting the job done right.

Warning 4.8: Adjust your projected renovation schedule to take into account social events and holidays. For instance, if your daughter is getting married in August, you're going to have a hard time interviewing architects that month. Similarly, if you're assuming you'll be able to sit down and chat with GCs during the third week of December, you're in for a disappointment.

5 Set your budget and figure out where the money is coming from.

Kitchen renovations cost roughly $10,000–$20,000 for a face-lift and $20,000–$35,000 for a basic remodeling. There are as many different ways to pay for this project as there are styles of cabinet knobs. Choosing the method you use is a decision that must be based on your personal financial situation and after consultations with your financial and tax advisers. That being said, there are some general tips and warnings I can offer you.

☐ **Done**

Tip 5.1: If your kitchen renovation is a minor job (i.e., a partial makeover) costing less than $8,000, my advice is not to go into debt for it. Either take the money out of your savings or make it a regular monthly budget item spread over a period of time—even if that means cutting your budget somewhere else (entertainment or travel, for example). The time, effort, and costs of borrowing wisely are too great to justify taking out such a small home renovation loan.

Tip 5.2: If revamping your kitchen is going to cost between $8,000 and $25,000, I'd suggest an installment loan. If the loan is secured by the home itself and is earmarked specifically for home renovation, it's called a home improvement loan. If it's unsecured and there's no stipulation as to how the money must be used, it's a personal loan.

Tip 5.3: You might apply for a new credit card with a very low introductory rate and use it to pay for the renovation. Be sure to note when the teaser rate expires and then transfer the balance to another card, again taking advantage of the low initial rate.

Tip 5.4: If the work on your kitchen is going to cost $25,000 or more, I'd suggest borrowing against the equity you have in your home. Simply put, your equity is equal to the difference between your home's current market value and the balance of your mortgage. Generally, home equity loans operate as lines of credit. You draw money as needed and interest accrues only on what you draw down.

Tip 5.5: Another way to pay for a kitchen renovation slated to cost $25,000 or more is to refinance your first mortgage. Most people think of mortgage refinancing as a way to decrease monthly payments, but it can also be used for "cashing out," or pulling equity money back out of the house.

Tip 5.6: No matter what type of financing you require, make sure to shop around for the best rates (ask for the APR) and terms.

FINDING AND CHOOSING SOMEONE TO DRAW YOUR PLANS

YOU may have extraordinary taste. You may be able to plan an incredible marketing program. You may get rave reviews for the sketches you bring to the lumberyard when you buy shelving. None of these mean you can draft your own kitchen plans. In order to ensure that this job goes smoothly you're going to need professionally drawn plans and specifications. Exactly whom you hire to come up with those blueprints depends on the type of project you're envisioning.

6 **Accept that you'll need a professionally drawn set of plans**. While the form and author of your formal plan will vary depending on the size and type of project, you shouldn't do without it even if you're having nothing more than a relatively minor face-lift done. Professionally drawn plans ensure that your wants and needs are defined. Formal plans also help ensure that the contractors' bids won't be out of line with your budget. They provide a framework that makes competitive bids easy to compare, analyze, and validate. And they represent the heart of the contract between you and your architect and between you and the GC.

☐ **Done**

Tip 6.1: The phrase "plans and specifications" refers to a wide range of forms. In the most general sense, it means the documents prepared by the architect, including individual papers known as plans, elevations, sections, detailing, and specifications. Plans are an overhead look at the floor plan. Specifications are a list of features that usually include weights, colors, sizes, and even brand names and model numbers of materials or fixtures. Elevations are ground-level views of the front, rear, and sides of the structure. Sections are cross-sectional views of your home, as seen through the house down a particular line. Details are sketches of ornamental or structural parts of the project—a special molding, for example. Depending upon what you're having done to your kitchen, your plans and specifications may include one or all of these elements.

Warning 6.2: Don't hire a contractor to execute both the plans and the renovation work. First of all, that strategy will prohibit competitive bidding on the project. And you also have a conflict of interest—a contractor might recommend changes that create more work than is necessary for what you want to accomplish.

7 Decide whom you need to draft plans and specifications.

The specific type of professional you hire to draft the plans and specifications for your kitchen renovation depends on the type of renovation you have in mind.

☐ **Done**

Tip 7.1: I tell my clients that they should use architects to plan all projects that require notification to the local building department and the issuance of a construction permit. You may not be able to obtain the required permits without the signature of a licensed architect on the plans. The requirement of an architect's signature varies with the municipality, but generally it is necessary when the renovation includes major structural changes. In other municipalities, the architect's signature is not necessary, but will certainly help smooth things along. Most architects charge a fee equal to about 10 percent of the total cost of the job for a complete set of plans and specifications. Preferably, he or she should be a member of the American Institute of Architects (AIA).

Tip 7.2: Interior designers are similar to architects: some even have architectural training, but have chosen to specialize in interiors. They are therefore qualified to provide guidance on such areas as room layout, furnishings, fixtures, cabinets, lighting, floor materials, and wall and ceiling finishes. The American Society of Interior Designers (ASID) grants certification to its members; so-called professional members are those who have passed an examination given by the National Council for Interior Design Qualification (NCIDQ) and who have four to five years training and at least two years of work experience.

Tip 7.3: There are also design professionals who use the designation "remodeler." They specialize in remodeling and have training and work experience exclusively in this area. Their credentials may include education and certification as a Certified Graduate Remodeler (CGR) given by the Remodelers Council of the National Association of Home Builders. Remodelers may also qualify for a Certified Remodeler (CR) designation for the National Association of the Remodeling Industry.

Tip 7.4: If your kitchen is having a cosmetic face-lift, you'll need an interior designer or a kitchen planner.

Tip 7.5: If possible, hire a specialized kitchen planner. While not schooled in interior design, they are certified by the National Kitchen and Bath Association (designated as Certified Kitchen Designer, CKD), and thus are well trained in the principles and products of kitchen and bath design. Independent planners usually charge between $35 to $50 per hour. But beware of planners with showroom affiliations—it may mean you will be limited to those brands, or at least pushed into buying certain ones.

Tip 7.6: The best way to find architects, designers, and kitchen planners is through word of mouth. You want recommendations from people who have done roughly the same type of kitchen renovation that you're planning.

Tip 7.7: Also, the American Institute of Architects, the National Kitchen and Bath Association, the National Association of Home Builders, the American Society of Interior Designers, and the National Association of the Remodeling Industry can all provide recommendations of architects or designers in your geographic vicinity.

Warning 7.8: Sometimes it's wise to run your list of names by your local building department. Do not hire a planner who is out of favor with the building department. Similarly, if you live in a condo or co-op, check your list with the managing agent or building board and steer clear of candidates they don't like.

8 **Interview each candidate on your list.** It's not enough to speak to candidates on the telephone. This individual is going to be responsible for planning renovations to the heart of your home and the most important space in your family's life. You need to meet with candidates in person to get a sense of who they are and whether they care.

☐ **Done**

Tip 8.1: Whichever of the professionals you interview, check to see whether they are members of their respective professional associations. This is especially important for the architect, because it means that person has the requisite training and experience and adheres to a certain standard. For the others it encourages accountability.

Tip 8.2: Not all of the architects you interview are going to be licensed. That shouldn't be a concern. The licensing exam is a killer and all it does is give the architect the right to sign and file official plans. If you're wondering what unlicensed architects do, then, when it comes time to file plans, I'll tell you: they simply turn to a licensed colleague and get him or her to sign them.

Tip 8.3: Ask each architect candidate how much of his or her work is residential and what percentage of it involves kitchen renovations. Make sure you find out if the individual you're talking to will be doing the actual work or will be turning it over to an associate or staffer.

Tip 8.4: Ask the architect about an hourly fee rather than one as a percentage of the total cost of the job. The hourly rate for services is generally between $55 and $150 an hour for an experienced architect, and especially for small jobs, this fee structure tends to be more economical. See if you can get the architect to agree to the lower of an hourly rate or 5 percent of the total. Additionally, arrange to be billed monthly and insist that the bill be itemized.

Tip 8.5: Ask how much experience the architect has with kitchens and especially how much experience with hands-on management. Double-check that he or she has experience dealing with the local building department, if a filing is required. Find out about fees and what services are included.

Tip 8.6: Whether you use an architect, planner, or designer, discuss your budget up front. Demonstrate how you came up with it and how you're determined to stick with it. If she protests that it is too restraining, or hems and haws about her ability to come within 15 percent of the figure you've proposed, thank her for her time and scratch her off your list.

Tip 8.7: Don't underestimate the importance of rapport when it comes to working with the architect or planner of your choice. Simply put, your wish should be her command when it comes to transforming your kitchen. You want someone who shows respect for your ideas and feelings, while being able to offer suggestions that enhance your tastes, not hers.

Warning 8.8 : Avoid the temptation to hire the current "hot" interior designer whose client list glitters with dropable names. While it might be fun to add your name to a register of the rich and famous, couture interior designers are likely to overlook your needs in order to design a kitchen that reflects their vision.

Tip 8.9: As with the architect, you want a kitchen designer or remodeler who is a specialist in the type—both budget-wise and stylewise—of kitchen you want.

Warning 8.10: Watch out for kitchen designers and planners who work exclusively for one retailer or supplier. The plans they come up with will be tailored along the product lines the store carries and wants to sell. The cost of the plans will also be tied to the purchase of products and services from the home center.

9 **Hire a construction manager to handle the hands-on, day-to-day supervision if your renovation is projected to cost over $125,000.** For a fee of between 3 to 5 percent of the total cost, or for between $75 to $100 an hour, he will take care of everything from negotiating the construction contracts to making sure the right materials are used and delivered on time.

☐ **Done**

Tip 9.1: Turn to your architect for names of reputable construction managers. When interviewing prospects, ask about relevant experience, services, and fees. If it's a toss-up between two, opt for the individual with the best background in residential renovation. That's important, since construction managers mostly work on commercial construction jobs.

Tip 9.2: Generally, your architect will conduct periodic inspections to confirm that the work is being done according to her plans. And she will make a final inspection when the work is complete, before you make the last payment. You can talk to your architect about providing periodic supervision instead of hiring a construction manager. This will add about 30–50 percent to the fee.

Warning 9.3: Architects love to put on a hard hat, but many are not experienced managers. On a really big job, you're better off hiring a separate construction manager. On a smaller job, the architect's regularly scheduled inspections will probably suffice.

Contracting and Collaborating with Your Planner

Having selected someone to draw blueprints for your project, you've now got to have a lawyer draw blueprints for this new relationship. Even though you're dealing with creative professionals, the rights and responsibilities of both parties must be detailed in a protective document. And having committed your relationship to paper, the two of you now have to work together and come up with plans that match your visions and budget.

10 **Contract with your planning professional.** Whichever professionals you choose to go with to develop your plans and specifications, you'll need to formalize the relationship in an enforceable contract.

☐ **Done**

Tip 10.1: Most architects and designers use the American Institute of Architects (AIA) standard form contract, which is pretty standard and straightforward. Still, don't be afraid to make changes. Bring the contract to your attorney to read. Independent space planners sometimes use an AIA form or have a custom form drafted.

Tip 10.2: The contract should spell out the responsibilities of the architect or planner. Fees, payment schedules, and ownership of plans and drawings are all negotiable and should be described in detail.

Tip 10.3: Without a doubt, the most important area of the contract is where the services to be rendered are specified. The design professional is not required to do anything that is not spelled out in the contract, so make sure it's all there in fine print, no matter how minor. You want to have the architect or kitchen planner to prepare preliminary studies, including alternative configurations of the renovation. And you want to be sure any changes in the plans that are necessary will be made. If there are to be visitations by the professional, it should be mentioned.

Tip 10.4: Make sure the terms under which the architect or planner is entitled to her fees are clearly stated. Pay only a small amount up front, another sum when the preliminary designs are done, and make the final payment only when the plans are completed to your satisfaction and approved by the building department, if necessary.

Tip 10.5: A clause should be added that details how your relationship with the planner can be terminated and what happens to the plans and drawings if it is. Also, include a clause about how fee disputes are to be resolved. Consider including an arbitration clause so that any full-blown disagreements that do arise will be resolved through arbitration—it's less time consuming and costly than litigation.

Tip 10.6: Construction managers usually have their own custom contracts. Since you'll be employing one only if your renovation is substantial (and expensive), definitely run it by your attorney to amend or add to as necessary.

11 **Work with your planning professional in developing the plans.** You've contracted with someone to draft your plans and supervise the job. Now is the time to roll up your sleeves and get down to the nitty-gritty: sit down with your planner and discuss exactly what you want and need.

☐ **Done**

Tip 11.1: Learn the art of patience. Don't expect to sit down over one cup of coffee with an architect, designer, or kitchen planner and come away an hour later with a set of plans. It's a process of give and take that can last anywhere from a few weeks to several months, depending upon what you're having done. Nothing really productive will start to happen until you are both talking the same language— so be careful about saying you understand the architect's lingo when you don't.

Warning 11.2: Don't worry if it seems to be taking the planner a long time to draw up the plans. She's actually saving you time and money, since a comprehensive set of plans minimizes the potential for surprises and added charges once the work has begun. Every extra day spent in planning saves a week in construction. And every extra dollar spent now saves ten dollars later on.

Tip 11.3: Make sure the specifications listed are as detailed as possible. For example: it shouldn't just say you want a new sink and new cabinets. Rather, it should include technical data, such as model number, style, color, etc. Also, be careful, because architects have a propensity to be preoccupied with looks and will throw geography to the wind—for example, shipping Vermont marble to San Diego. You'll always save money if the materials are manufactured and sold within your region, not just because shipping is less costly, but if there are errors, they are much easier to rectify.

Tip 11.4: Specificity should be the operative term when discussing sketches and plans with your planner. But at the same time, don't be afraid to offer abstract criticism, such as the feeling that a room is too "heavy." A pro should know what concrete elements contribute to your feeling that way and adjust the plans accordingly.

Warning 11.5: Watch out for architects, designers, or planners who try to increase the scope of a proposed renovation project once they've started on the job and become "excited about it."

Tip 11.6: Take the time to study the plan and mull it over before submitting it for bids. A month isn't too long for you and your family to let it percolate. If you're having a hard time envisioning the renovation, pay the extra money for a model or a set of 3-D interior drawings.

12 Spend time studying your plans.

The more time you take to think about and study your plans, the more likely they'll be complete, and the more satisfied you'll be with the outcome. Indulge in a little creative visualization, picturing yourself in your kitchen after the work has been done. Think about all the things you do in the kitchen over the course of the day. Have you forgotten anything? Also, think about the logical flow of the room and what appliances you might like to have next to each other. How many steps does it take to go from stove to sink? Can this process be made simpler? How do the doors of appliances open? Is there room to walk around them when they are open?

☐ **Done**

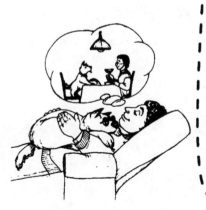

Tip 12.1: Consider your kitchen's current location in your home. Is it centrally located? Can you get groceries from the car to the kitchen without either the bags breaking or you tripping through an obstacle course of doorways? Maybe you want to swap the current kitchen location with that of another room—if you spend more time here than anywhere else, a large living/dining room space might better be used as a living room/kitchen.

Tip 12.2: Since the kitchen gets so much traffic, you might think more entrances to the room, the better. Not necessarily. Eliminating an entryway creates wall space that can translate into additional space for cabinets or even an eating area.

Warning 12.3: The classic kitchen design is focused on the work triangle—that is the area defined by the stove, sink, and refrigerator. The relationship between these three areas is essential for the cook—the movement among them should be unobstructed. Be careful about the placement of islands or appliances that interrupt that flow.

Tip 12.4: A good kitchen design focuses on details. So no matter which element you are discussing at any one moment (cabinets, floors, counters), be sure to think about the treatment of edges, moldings, and hardware. The small touches are what give the room character and style—and let you achieve a more expensive look for less money.

Tip 12.5: Design your new kitchen with the present and future in mind. If you have small children, remember that they play on the floor and get into lower drawers and cabinets. You can provide for toy storage at that level and/or latches for cabinets that you want them to stay out of. And don't forget, the kids will grow up, and while you'll always be young at heart, you'll grow up too—so think about how your needs may change over time.

Tip 12.6: A walk-in pantry is a real plus if you have the space or can add it. It should be cooler than the rest of the kitchen and if you want to store large platters, fish poachers, and pots and pans that have limited or seasonal usage, the shelves should be adjustable.

13 **Choose cabinets to set the tone for your kitchen.** Cabinets are the principal design element of the kitchen. And except for the labor costs of the planner and contractor, the cabinets are the most expensive item that will go into your kitchen. The ultimate cost-saving strategy is to reface existing cabinets, but that works only if you are not also reconfiguring the room.

☐ **Done**

Tip 13.1: If your planner suggests using expensive solid-wood cabinets, you could suggest substituting cabinets with solid-wood fronts but particleboard interiors—they're much more affordable.

Tip 13.2: Believe it or not, custom cabinets and countertops made on the job are often less costly than those you can get in a showroom or through mail order. The big cabinet companies are very expensive and off-the-rack cabinets often need extra work because they may not quite fit in their prefabricated form.

Warning 13.3: Beware of purchasing cabinets that don't come with supports in all four corners. They do not provide the structural integrity you will want.

Tip 13.4: Make sure your contractor carefully checks the cabinets you ordered when they arrive. You want the manufacturer to correct any problems such as warped doors or mismatched pieces before your contractor begins installation.

Warning 13.5: Irregularities in your floors or walls can affect how the cabinets are hung and whether doors and drawers line up and open and close correctly. Make sure the installer (or your contractor) takes these irregularities into account before the cabinets are hung.

14

Be aware that the appliances you choose will impact the cost of the job and the look of your kitchen. Be truthful about how often you cook and your level of cooking skill. You don't want kitchen equipment that is inappropriate for you. And remember, the more elaborate the appliances, the more expensive they are.

☐ **Done**

Warning 14.1: Not only are restaurant-caliber appliances more expensive than ordinary consumer appliances, but installing them is likely to be more complicated and costly. Larger appliances often demand more electric or gas power, which means a bigger line. Also, more insulation is often required, as well as professional ventilations and fire-suppression systems. And watch out for residential restaurant lines. Some companies have caught on to consumers' fascination with restaurant-style appliances and have created lines to suit residential installation. They are priced astronomically.

Tip 14.2: Separating the oven from the range allows you to put the oven higher up, which is more convenient when you're cooking—but separating them takes up more space.

Tip 14.3: Think about where small appliances will go. Do you want them scattered about on all the countertops or together in an appliance "garage"—a closed storage area on the counter in which small appliances can be kept out of the way, yet handy? Consider space-saver small appliances that are hung underneath cabinets.

Tip 14.4: If you entertain a lot or have your extended family over every holiday, one dishwasher may not be enough. Placing two dishwashers away from the main cooking area works well.

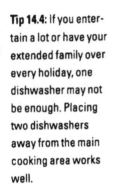

Warning 14.5: Be careful about placement of the oven and dishwasher. You want to have room to walk around when the doors are open. In a small kitchen with these appliances on opposite walls, be sure there is enough room to open both at once without trapping yourself.

Warning 14.6: A glass door on the refrigerator requires too much effort to keep looking clean and in some kind of order. You'll always feel compelled to arrange the contents so they line up neatly. A fridge with a stainless-steel door is preferable.

Tip 14.7: If more than one member of the household cooks at a time, a double sink with vegetable prep utility compartment can be useful. You may also consider putting in a second sink. The two sinks should be about ten feet apart to allow two people to work comfortably (without stepping on each other's toes).

15

Realize that the countertops you pick must serve two purposes—visual and functional. Like cabinetry and appliances, the counters are a visual element of the kitchen. But they also take the most abuse. You want them to be pretty; however, they must also be able to resist stains, heat damage, warping, and scratches—and be easy to keep clean.

☐ **Done**

Tip 15.1: Good quality countertop materials are a better buy in the long run. Also, there is no reason to settle for one countertop material. You could opt for butcher block, stainless steel, granite, Formica, or any combination. For example, you can put stainless steel next to the stove for hot pots and pans, and butcher block elsewhere, except next to the sink, where you'll want a waterproof surface. Also, set-ins give you added flexibility. In other words, inset a butcher-block cutting board into a Formica countertop or create a built-in trivet by insetting ceramic tile.

Tip 15.2: Granite countertops look great—but watch out. They tend to chip and can't be repaired. But if you're sold on this surface, you can save money by installing a built-up edge. That means a granite border makes the counter appear to be solid granite, but the top piece is only half as thick and mounted on a wooden base.

Tip 15.3: Areas around sinks need waterproof surfaces. Don't use wood, because it soaks up liquid, which causes it to expand and warp. Stone is the best material to use. And consider a one-piece sink unit—sink, backsplash, and a foot or so of counter on each side—the absence of seams makes it easier to maintain.

Tip 15.4: The height of the counter is often "standard." But there is no reason not to customize the height at a level comfortable for you. The counter for chopping should be calibrated to your arm length. Also, different heights may be appropriate for different work spaces. Just be aware that any variations from the "standard" may make your home harder to sell.

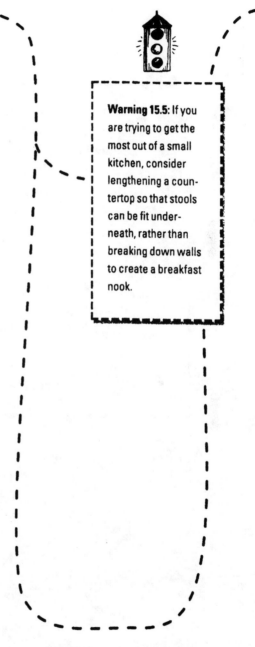

Warning 15.5: If you are trying to get the most out of a small kitchen, consider lengthening a countertop so that stools can be fit underneath, rather than breaking down walls to create a breakfast nook.

16 Take into account all features when choosing your flooring, not just the price.

Since cooking is done while standing, the flooring should be as easy on the legs and back as possible. And if you have small children who'll be playing on the floor, softer surfaces might be more appropriate. But if your children are grown and you like to entertain (so that you always have guests in the kitchen), you might want to consider ceramic tile, which tends to have a richer, more stylish look.

☐ **Done**

Tip 16.1: Some floor material—stone, for example—is uncomfortable to stand on for long periods of time. Wood is better—but better yet, a new version of linoleum called marmoleum. Not only is it easier on the legs and back, but it comes in sheets that can be cut and the pieces welded together to create intricate patterns.

Tip 16.2: Don't shy away from what appear to be expensive vinyl floors. Cheap brands are more apt to scuff and tear. Tile, of course, is sturdier, but it is generally more expensive and can be harder to clean because dirt gets into the grout.

17

Don't forget that lighting is an essential tool in a kitchen. Proper light for a kitchen is one of the most important features. Your kitchen plan should account for both natural and artificial light. And, again, you need to accommodate your own needs. Cooks work with potentially dangerous kitchen implements, such as knives, and require adequate illumination for these tasks. Dual-career families who tend to gather in the kitchen after dark should forgo the skylight in favor of fixtures that will provide enough light to take dinner out of the freezer and put it into the microwave, and to do homework or read the paper by, while also establishing a cozy atmosphere.

☐ **Done**

Tip 17.1: Mixing fluorescent and incandescent lighting is the best way to achieve general illumination and at the same time brighten task areas.

Tip 17.2: In general, lighting should be indirect. Track lighting is a good bet for this reason. Also it is affordable and comes in many different styles.

Warning 17.3: Resist the temptation to buy recessed lighting fixtures. They may be unobtrusive and inexpensive, but they also provide only limited illumination. Also, they produce heat and so are uncomfortable to stand under.

Warning 17.4: Placement of lighting fixtures is extremely important. Light coming over your shoulder casts shadows on the countertops and makes cooking jobs a real chore. Under-the-cabinet supplemental task lighting is a good way to avoid the shadow problem.

18

Don't forget that adequate ventilation is very important. If you like to grill food on the stove top or broil it in the oven, you'll need a professional-size hood over the stove to capture the smoke.

☐ **Done**

19

Be aware that the color scheme you choose will have an impact on the look of your kitchen. Color affects the mood of the room as well as the perception of its size. An all-white kitchen makes the space look larger than it is and also reflects the light, which means a brighter kitchen overall. Consider warm earth tones and terra cottas—these lighter shades have an effect similar to white, but are not so stark. Also, you'll want to stick to a medium color range for the counters because darker colors tend to show scratches and dust more readily.

☐ **Done**

FINDING AND CHECKING UP ON CANDIDATE CONTRACTORS

The individual who's most responsible for the success or failure of your kitchen renovation isn't you or your planner. It's your GC. He's the one who has to turn the ideas you've developed and drafted into dining nooks and drawers. It's his responsibility to turn dreams into reality and, in the process, keep you from being bankrupted. Because so much is riding on this one person, you must make every effort to ensure that your slate of candidates is a good one.

20 Decide if you need a traditional GC or a specialist. In theory, GCs should be able to handle any type of work. A specialist GC is one who prefers to deal in one type of renovation only, such as kitchens.

☐ **Done**

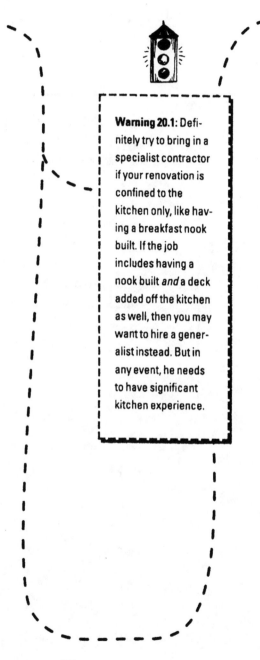

Warning 20.1: Definitely try to bring in a specialist contractor if your renovation is confined to the kitchen only, like having a breakfast nook built. If the job includes having a nook built *and* a deck added off the kitchen as well, then you may want to hire a generalist instead. But in any event, he needs to have significant kitchen experience.

21 **If you're going with a generalist contractor, decide which kind you need.** Some contractors are extremely upscale, working out of offices that boast a staff of architects, designers, carpenters, etc. Others are mainly renovators who work from home and whom you can count on to turn up at the job site daily. Finally, there are those contractors who do everything, including their own carpentry, and list the cab of their pickup truck as their office. You need to figure out which one is right for you.

☐ **Done**

Tip 21.1: The hotshot with a large staff probably won't come in with a budget under $100,000 because he can't afford to, the renovator will most likely only take jobs that fall in the middle, and the hands-on guy probably can't afford to take on a major project even if he has the skill to handle it.

Warning 21.2: GCs will look at your project and think about two things: how much it will cost them, and if it's worth the time spent.

22 Develop a list of candidate contractors.

The best way to come up with a list of possible GCs is to get expert advice: go to your architect, interior designer, construction manager, or kitchen planner.

☐ **Done**

Warning 22.1: Avoid the temptation to solicit recommendations from relatives, neighbors, and friends, as well as words of wisdom from paint stores, home centers, and lumberyards. The former will simply tell you whom they've used—they've no idea whether or not they're right for your job, and the latter will give you the names of their customers.

Tip 22.2: When asking for recommendations, stress that you're looking for the best person for the job, not the cheapest. You want your architect or planner to get along with the contractor so that the job of renovating your kitchen becomes a team project rather than a battle of titanic egos.

Tip 22.3: Finding local contractors through a social network is okay. It means that if they do poor work, they know it will get around. You want them to feel that their reputation in the community is at stake because it gives them incentive to complete the job to your satisfaction in the hope you'll tell others.

Tip 22.4: It can't hurt to run the names you get past the local building department or a member of the co-op board or homeowners association. Using a GC who gets thumbs up from the bureaucracy you'll be dealing with later on could be an advantage if any problems develop down the line.

23 **Set up the bidding procedure.** Buy yourself three file folders—one for each GC you plan to interview and ask to submit a bid—and put a complete set of plans and specifications in each. Telephone your three top candidates, explain who you are, say who recommended them, and describe what you're looking for. Make an appointment for each to come to your house.

☐ **Done**

Tip 23.1: There are lots of licensed, insured, reputable contractors out there who only work part-time, conducting their business on weekends and in the evenings because they work full-time jobs during the day. These contractors offer the incentive of reasonable pricing. It's definitely worth checking them out if you don't mind having your kitchen being demolished while you are trying to watch television or while you're having Sunday brunch. But if you live in a co-op or condo, check your building rules—they may not allow you to have work done after hours or on weekends.

24 **Take charge when you meet with your GC candidates.** Contractors are salesmen like anyone else: don't let them sell you. Instead, set the correct tone right from the start by demonstrating you're the one in control.

☐ **Done**

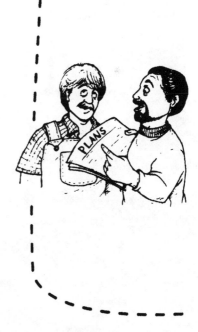

Tip 24.1: Show who's boss by handing each contractor a set of plans and specifications when he arrives. Don't be afraid to let him see you have three folders. It can only help if he knows you're talking to other contractors. If anything, it'll keep him on his toes. Explain you're looking for a fixed or budget price.

Warning 24.2: Some contractors might suggest following a pricing scheme based on actual time and materials plus profit and overhead. Don't do it! The only person this benefits is the contractor, since it ensures he won't lose money on the job. Working this way also has a tendency to lead to both time and cost overruns. Asking for a budget price forces the contractor to come up with accurate cost estimates. And it forces him to shop around among subs to get the best prices for the plumbing, electrical, and other work.

Tip 24.3: Don't be surprised if the contractor says he'll have to boost his bid up by 10 to 20 percent if you want a budget price. To offset this surcharge, say you'll offer a bonus if the job comes in under budget and ahead of schedule. You can offer to split any cost savings with the contractor. On the flip side, don't hesitate to add penalties for delays.

Tip 24.4: Never let the cat out of the bag and say what your proposed budget is. If the GC knows you're prepared to shell out $70,000, he won't come in with a bid for any less.

Tip 24.5: Ask for the bids to be broken down by individual trades, the better to spot any problems with subs prior to commissioning the job. You always want the option of asking the contractor to go back and get a price from a less expensive sub if the one quoted is too high. Also, explain that you plan to comparison-shop the appliances and will agree to purchase them from the GC only if he agrees to share his professional discount with you.

Tip 24.6: Make sure you ask all candidates to mention how much they charge for add-ons—such as installing an extra electrical or telephone outlet or relocating a plumbing or lighting fixture. Make a list of all the possible extras you can and get prices for these items in advance. If you wait until work is well under way, the GC may charge as much as twice the normal fee—that could be because the work is more difficult or because he wants to complete his work and get out and changes lengthen the term of the project. Also, he's gotcha.

Tip 24.7: Invite the candidates to make suggestions if they come across anything in the plans that outrages their sensibilities either in terms of practicality or cost. Ask them to indicate if there are any areas where they could save you money by altering plans or if they find any gaps or mistakes in the plans and how they should be corrected. Also, tell them if they come up with something they think would enhance the project, they should feel free to list it separately as well as the effect it would have on the bottom line. Finally, have them include anything they think might come up, based on their experience, that they don't see in the plans—I'm thinking specifically of how they handle "surprises" that arise when walls are opened up. Insist that all this information be listed separately from the bid.

Tip 24.8: Be sure you ask the candidates to include all "soft costs" when working up their estimates. Soft costs are expenses such as permit fees, etc., that aren't directly related to materials and labor.

Tip 24.9: Have the GC also include a price for demolition of your existing kitchen and debris removal. If the cost is based on the number of Dumpsters used, make sure there is a cap on that number and that you get credit for unused loads. Also, you might want to be sure that debris will be removed in an environmentally sound way.

Tip 24.10: Don't forget to plan for the inevitable inconveniences when discussing the job with potential contractors. Cooking in your kitchen may be out of the question for anywhere from a few days to a few months, and you definitely want to be sure you've cleared out the cabinets and appliances well before the crew shows up for work the first day. Ask the contractor to explain the sequence of events, and see if you can come up with a guesstimate as to how long your kitchen will be unusable. If you have to, write out the sequence of events to better anticipate and avoid complications.

Tip 24.11: Talk to the contractor about helping you set up a temporary kitchen in the living room, or even the garage—and what he might charge to do it. You'll need enough power to run the microwave and toaster oven as well as a hot plate and possibly even the refrigerator. Of course, you have other options—eating out, wangling invitations from friends. Or think about "camping out" in the family room with camping gear that might include a hot pot and pressure cooker. You can even buy dehydrated foods that do not need to be refrigerated. Also stock up on paper goods, because washing dishes may be problematic.

25 **Get homeowner references.** Ask the contractors for the names of three jobs they've done that resemble yours, so you can check out their workmanship. Tell them you want one from this year, one from last year, and one from the year previous to that. Most GCs won't be able to reel this information off the top of their head, so give them a few days to get back to you. When they do, add the information to your folders.

☐ **Done**

Warning 25.1: Don't trust any contractor who discourages you from visiting previous work sites or suggests that photos can serve as evidence of his work.

26 Get financial references.

Ask each candidate to provide you with a bank reference and a business reference, and to include a copy of his credit file in the bidding package. If any of them refuse, scratch them off your list. When you get the information, add it to your folders.

☐ **Done**

27 **Contact the Better Business Bureau.** As the third GC pulls out of your driveway, get on the horn to the Better Business Bureau, and ask if they have information—positive or negative—about your three candidates. Repeat the request with the nearest office of your state's department of consumer affairs or the consumer protection agency. Record all information you receive.

☐ **Done**

Warning 27.1: Don't get upset if there are a couple of complaints on file for all of your candidates. Almost every businessperson at one time or another has a disagreement with a customer. Try to get some details about the complaints so you can ask the contractor about them later on. (So what if he thinks you're a snoop? All you're doing is showing that you mean business.) Find out if the number of complaints is less, more, or average for the trade.

28 **Check the candidates' legal status.** Contact your attorney and ask her to find out if there are any liens or judgments against any of the candidates. Any suits filed or judgments obtained by unhappy customers or suppliers will be a matter of public record. This will cost you from $75 to $100. When you get the information, add it to your folders. This will give you additional information otherwise not available in a credit file.

☐ **Done**

Tip 28.1: If yours is a big project (over $25,000) ask your attorney to obtain a Dun & Bradstreet report on each contractor. This is a financial synopsis of the company that contains background on the corporate officers and a description of the company's credit history. Expect to pay between $300 and $600 for it (if your banker subscribes, you may be able to get a D&B report for a nominal charge). If you are unable to obtain a D&B report, ask your attorney or banker to run a personal credit report on the principal owner.

29 **Check the financial references.** Telephone the business and bank references given you by the contractors. Explain who you are and that you wish to make sure the contractor in question is both reliable and financially sound. Note any comments, positive or negative, in your folders.

☐ **Done**

30 Interview each homeowner reference your candidates have provided.

Ask each reference:

• Did the project begin and proceed on schedule?

• Did the GC crew work every day until the job was completed?

• Was the crew punctual?

• Did the crew clean up at the end of the day?

• Did the crew work a full day?

• How many breaks did the crew take during the day? Were the breaks excessive?

• Did you have any problems with the building department?

• Did the job come in on schedule and within budget?

• Were you easily able to contact the GC to discuss problems or changes?

• Did the GC always appear to need his next payment desperately?

• Was the work properly coordinated? Did crew have to wait for materials or guidance?

- Who was the site foreman and should I request him specifically?
- Did the GC pay the subs in a timely manner? Were there any mechanic's liens filed against your property?
- Did you encounter any problems after the job was "finished"? How big was the "punch list"?
- If so, did the GC come back to resolve the problems? How long did it take him?

When you return home from your interviews with the references, put your notes on the homeowners' answers to your questions in the proper file.

☐ **Done**

Tip 30.1: Stick to yes-or-no questions if you can. Remember: you don't want opinions, you want facts.

31 **Judge the quality of the workmanship.** While interviewing the references, look around for signs of how good a job was done. Realize that you'll actually be judging the work of subs. Still, the odds are good the GC will use many of the same people on your project.

☐ **Done**

Tip 31.1: Much of the work being done on your kitchen will involve finish carpentry, the detail work of building cabinets and installing interior window trim, interior doors and trim, and moldings.

• Look for neat cuts and tight joints. You should not be able to detect any saw or hammer marks, and the margins between doors and their frames should be even all the way around.
• Pay special attention to the corner joints of moldings: a good carpenter will make sure there's no visible gap.
• Cabinets should be screwed into the wall, not nailed.

Tip 31.2: When it comes to interior painting, look for these signs of outstanding work:

• even coats with no signs of brush marks or roller nap
• no visible repairs
• even lines where the gloss paint on trim meets the matte paint on walls or ceilings, or where two different colors meet
• neatly painted window frames with paint in the joint where the glass meets the wood—but not on the pane itself

Tip 31.3: To determine the skill of a wallpaper hanger, check out how he handled switch and outlet plates. A good paperhanger will cover the plates with scrap paper, making sure the patterns match on the wall.

Tip 31.4: When it comes to flooring, the signs of good workmanship are:

- equal borders on all sides
- no gaps between walls or cabinets and the flooring
- a centrally located pattern

- even margins around obstructions like radiator pipes
- flooring that extends under major appliances
- tight, flat, straight seams in unobtrusive areas

Tip 31.5: The signs of good workmanship when it comes to floor tiles include:

- symmetrical layouts in which the outside tiles are all approximately the same size
- a level surface
- uncracked and sealed grout that's between the tiles

Tip 31.6: One sign of a professionally laid wooden floor is that you're unable to detect a single nail head. The exception to the invisible nail mark of excellence is when the homeowner is going for a more rustic look. In this case, some combination of blind and face nailing is usually employed, with the face nailing being done with decorative forged nails.

Tip 31.7: Since most of the work done by plumbers and electricians is hidden from the eye, you're not going to be able to make a judgment on the quality of the subs' work. However, it's safe to assume that a GC who uses excellent carpenters, painters, paperhangers, and tile and flooring installers, will also use excellent plumbers and electricians. This is one instance when you can generally judge a book by its cover.

Analyzing Bids and Choosing Your GC

The fact that all your candidate GCs are bidding on the same set of detailed plans and specifications will help to ensure that you won't be comparing apples with oranges when the bids come back. But that doesn't mean all you have to do is pick the lowest price and sign on the dotted line. A bid is a complicated document that contains, between the lines, a very detailed story about both your candidates and the people they'll be hiring to do the actual hammering and nailing in your kitchen.

32 **Accept the bids from the contractor candidates.** By the time you're done with all your phoning and legwork, the GCs will probably be done with their bids and will want to drop them off. Let them. It will give them a chance to explain their calculations. Just be aware, though, that they'll also be trying to sell you. Listen to what each has to say, but remain non-committal. Thank them for their efforts, and inform them you'll be getting back to them as soon as you have a chance to look over the bids.

☐ **Done**

Tip 32.1: When you receive the bid, ask the contractor to initial the plans as proof he was working from them. This could come in handy later should there be a dispute.

Tip 32.2: Also, ask some questions:

• Did the GC find any problems with the plans?

• Did the GC obtain bids from more than one subcontractor for each of the different jobs of the kitchen renovation?

• How long has the GC known the subcontractors whose bids he used?

• How was each number of the bids derived? What's cost? What's profit?

33

Learn a little about the way bids are put together. In order to compare bids and make an informed, intelligent decision, you first need to understand how they're put together. Using your set of plans and specs, the GC can pretty accurately determine the size and scope of the job from the start. He'll have a sense of the job and cost breakdown by trade. He'll then contact the various subcontractors, provide each with a set of plans, and ask each to come up with a price. Each individual sub will price out his part of the job, including the fixtures and materials he'll need. The GC also factors in the costs of laborers required to do the "noncraft" work, such as demolition, debris removal, delivery and unloading of materials, and cleaning up. He can then actually calculate a subtotal for all the subcontracted work. To that number he adds his overhead and profit (averaging 10–20 percent) and that is the total price, or in other words, the final bill.

☐ **Done**

34

Read the bids line by line— looking at the bottom line isn't enough. If you're like most people, the first thing you'll want to check out are the bottom lines of the bids. That's okay—in fact, if your plans describe the job well, each bid should come within 15 percent of your own budget. When the bids cluster within 5–10 percent of each other, then you can feel confident that the plans accurately describe the job. But if all the contractors come in higher than you expected, you may have to pare down the plans. And if there is a wide disparity in the bids, it may mean a problem with the plans (not clear or specific enough) or that one of the subcontractors' bids is inconsistent with the others. You'll only be able to identify this disparity by a careful line-by-line review of the bids.

☐ **Done**

Tip 34.1: Sub bids may be out of step with each other for a variety of reasons. Often, the sub is bidding only because of his loyalty to that GC, but doesn't really want the job. He'll throw out a high number figuring it won't be accepted, but that if it is, he'll make out well.

Tip 34.2: Look for possible substitutes among the subcontractors. That is, if you like GC A because he has the best references and reputation, but his bid is high, see if you can get him to switch subs. You can replace the high-priced plumber in A's bid with the lower-priced plumber in B's bid—so you get the GC you want and stay in your price range!

Tip 34.3: On the other hand, don't be surprised if some of the sub bids are totally identical. It's to be expected: the GCs may have gone to the same subs.

Tip 34.4: If one GC failed to account for a necessary trade, or, conversely, if only one of your three candidate contractors sees the need to bring in a particular trade, flag that line of the bid. Either the GC has made a mistake, spotted something the others missed, or—and this isn't pleasant to think about—has added an unnecessary expense to your bill. You'll find out which it is when you speak with him later on.

Tip 34.5: Examine the GCs' fees. Assuming they all do the same type of jobs, their overheads should be pretty close. Any differences in their figures reflects a hunger to do the job, so you'd do well to remember that it's the eager beaver who usually works the hardest.

35

Realize that your plans might be the source of problems. If every candidate comes in with a bid higher than your budget, it's your plans that are at fault. If that is indeed the case, call all the contractors, tell them what has happened, apologize profusely, and explain that you'll get back to them with amended plans within a week. Then, call your planning professional and read her the riot act, expressing your annoyance and stressing the need for another set of plans closer to the cost level originally requested. Point out any cost-cutting suggestions the contractor candidates might have made in their bids. When you receive the new—and, hopefully, improved—set of plans, call your GC candidates back and ask for new bids.

☐ **Done**

Warning 35.1: Even though this mix-up might cost you additional design fees, resist the temptation to fire your planning professional. Switching professionals at this point could set the project back two months or more.

Tip 35.2: If you have to cut back on your project, opt to narrow its scope rather than cut corners and skimp on quality. It's better to do a few things right rather than many things poorly.

36

Find out about any questionable items. Call your GC candidates to ask about any items you've flagged. If you don't get a plausible reason for each discrepancy, ask for another price.

☐ **Done**

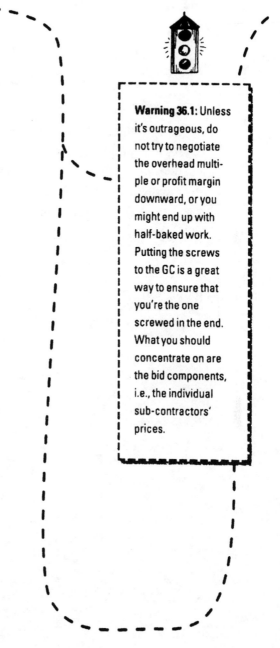

Warning 36.1: Unless it's outrageous, do not try to negotiate the overhead multiple or profit margin downward, or you might end up with half-baked work. Putting the screws to the GC is a great way to ensure that you're the one screwed in the end. What you should concentrate on are the bid components, i.e., the individual sub-contractors' prices.

37 **Have your planner check the bids.** Have your planning professional take a look at the bids, and ask her to double-check that the GCs have all followed specifications. Ask her to pay special attention to the lowest bidder, filling her in on all you know about the candidate's financial status. Don't forget to mention what you saw and found from visiting past jobs.

☐ **Done**

38 Select a GC. After taking into account experience, skill, motivation, and cost, select the contractor you want for the job.

☐ **Done**

Warning 38.1: Don't choose a contractor because he gives you a warm, fuzzy feeling and you think he likes you. Instead, try to keep your attention focused on which candidate is most likely to do a good job as well as finish on time and on budget.

Tip 38.2: Far be it from me to tell you whom to pick to work on your house. But if you don't mind my putting my two cents in, I'd have to say that if the lowest bidder is competent, solvent, seems to understand the job, and has good management skills, go with him.

CONTRACTING WITH YOUR CONTRACTOR

You were scrupulous in your search for the right contractor. But finding him and shaking hands on it isn't enough—you must put your agreement in writing in order to protect yourself.

Warning 39.1: Having a contract drawn up or even amending a form contract will cost you money. Depending on the scope of the job, the terms can become more complicated and so the contract will take more time to draft. On average expect to pay $300–$1,000. But you may be able to cut this cost if you let the contractor supply the contract and then have your attorney review it and make necessary changes.

Tip 39.2: Any kitchen job can really be a battlefield. The potential disputes are infinite. A good contract is a clear statement of everybody's obligations as well as a method of resolving disputes. So money spent on a contract is well worth it.

Warning 39.1: Having a contract drawn up or even amending a form contract will cost you money. Depending on the scope of the job, the terms can become more complicated and so the contract will take more time to draft. On average expect to pay $300–$1,000. But you may be able to cut this cost if you let the contractor supply the contract and then have your attorney review it and make necessary changes.

Tip 39.2: Any kitchen job can really be a battlefield. The potential disputes are infinite. A good contract is a clear statement of everybody's obligations as well as a method of resolving disputes. So money spent on a contract is well worth it.

Warning 39.3: Many GCs think their bidding forms are sufficient as contracts. That's fine for them, but these forms are vague at best and offer virtually no protection for you, the consumer. Also, the small print on the back oozes exculpation.

Warning 39.4: Some contractors do go one step further and use a standard form contract developed by the American Institute of Architects, but again, these forms simply aren't sufficient.

Tip 39.5: If the cost of your kitchen renovation project is too low to justify the expense of having a contract drafted, ask your attorney if she'll amend the AIA form instead. That, too, will cost money—most likely between $75 and $100—but it's less than having a contract drawn up from scratch. This form may be okay to use for larger jobs too.

Tip 39.6: When amending an AIA contract, make sure commencement and completion dates are inserted, as well as a clause imposing penalties of a specified amount for each day beyond the completion date. You probably should also add a clause providing a bonus for early completion to convince the GC to agree to the former.

40 **Make sure your contract is comprehensive.** What should your contract include? Among other things, a thorough discussion of all financial terms, including the total price, the down payment, when further payments are to be made, and how large they'll be.

☐ **Done**

Tip 40.1: You need to tie payments contractually to specific stages of the job. For example: the contract should state when 25 percent of the work has been completed, X amount of dollars will be paid; when 50 percent is done, Y amount of money will be handed over; and so on. These percentage plateaus can be described by the architect.

Typical installment milestones could be:

• preliminary framing, plumbing, and electrical inspections
• cabinet and flooring installation
• trim work, painting, and appliances
• final completion and building department sign-offs
• delivery of warranties, guarantees, punch-list completion, etc.

Tip 40.4: Make sure there's a clause stipulating no final moneys will be paid out until your supervisory professional or a representative of the municipality inspects the work done and certifies it is in accordance with local codes and regulations.

Tip 40.5: Make sure the contract ensures you remain ahead of the contractor at all times. In other words, you want him to have done more work and/or supplied more materials than he has actually been paid for. To achieve this, your contract should make clear you'll be keeping a 5 to 10 percent retainage. This means you'll be withholding this percent of each payment, including the final one, until thirty days after your supervisory professional certifies the job is finished. This ensures you'll have some leverage should you need the GC to come back and correct any problems.

Tip 40.6: Add a clause stipulating the job will be "continuously prosecuted." This means the job will continue uninterrupted and the GC won't start another project that interferes with the timely progress of the renovation.

Tip 40.7: The contract should also have a clause requiring the GC to obtain, as well as maintain, adequate insurance coverage. Ask the GC to show you an insurance certificate from his insurer that names you as a beneficiary. Ask your broker to review the document. You want to be certain the GC has enough liability insurance to cover any damage caused by him or any of the subs, and enough to cover any injury sustained by anyone working on the renovation project.

Tip 40.6: Add a clause stipulating the job will be "continuously prosecuted." This means the job will continue uninterrupted and the GC won't start another project that interferes with the timely progress of the renovation.

Tip 40.7: The contract should also have a clause requiring the GC to obtain, as well as maintain, adequate insurance coverage. Ask the GC to show you an insurance certificate from his insurer that names you as a beneficiary. Ask your broker to review the document. You want to be certain the GC has enough liability insurance to cover any damage caused by him or any of the subs, and enough to cover any injury sustained by anyone working on the renovation project.

Tip 40.8: At the same time, discuss your own insurance coverage. In the event the GC's policy turns out not to be sufficient, you'll want to be protected. Generally, the liability coverage that is part of your homeowner's policy won't be adequate—you'll need to supplement with an excess liability policy (which you should have had anyway).

Tip 40.9: If you find out that your GC's insurance will be up for renewal during the period he's to be working on your house, add a stipulation to the contract requiring him to provide proof of renewal as of the day of cancellation. Make it clear that no further moneys will be paid until such proof is provided.

Tip 40.10: Although substitutions of material of the same quality and cost are generally okay, make sure the agreement specifies that you'll be informed if such substitutions are to take place.

Tip 40.11: Another provision in the contract should state that you or your supervisory professional will be provided proof that the material suppliers and subs are actually being paid by the GC. This is crucial: in many states, if a sub or supplier isn't paid by the GC, he can file a mechanic's lien on your home and you will be liable for payment even though you have already paid the GC.

Tip 40.12: Ask your attorney about adding a "release of lien" clause. This requires the GC and subs to provide you with a waiver of lien, meaning they can't obtain a lien on your home if you fail to pay. This is especially important to get from the subs, because it protects you if the GC doesn't pay them on time or at all.

Tip 40.13: Make sure your contract discusses start and finish dates. An approximate date of completion will suffice, provided you include an absolute outside end-date—"not later than." Just be sure you include penalties and bonuses for late or early completion.

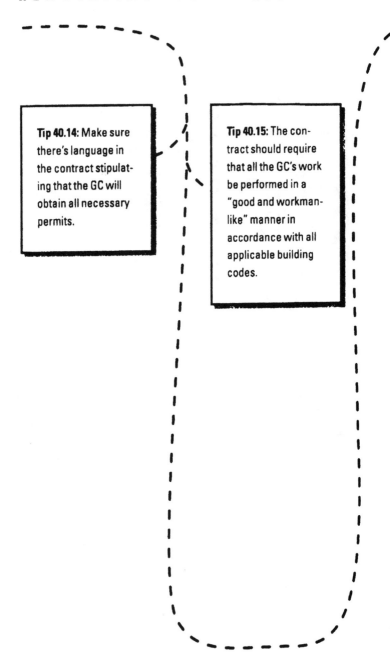

Tip 40.14: Make sure there's language in the contract stipulating that the GC will obtain all necessary permits.

Tip 40.15: The contract should require that all the GC's work be performed in a "good and workmanlike" manner in accordance with all applicable building codes.

Tip 40.16: If you want the GC to be responsible for cleaning up, removing debris, and protecting uninstalled materials, it had better say so in your contract. Incidentally, most contracts say "broom clean," but that's not enough. You'll want to specify that the cleaning be thorough—closer to "mint condition" than "broom clean."

Tip 40.17: While it's not pleasant to think about the possibility of you and your GC having a falling out, it can happen. To protect yourself, make sure the contract states that any irreconcilable differences must be resolved by the American Arbitration Association or through the auspices of the National Association of Home Builders. Modify the clause to provide that, in the event of arbitration, the "prevailing party" shall be entitled to recover its reasonable legal fees and expenses incurred in the arbitration. This will put "bite" in the clause and keep the contractor honest.

Tip 40.18: There should be an entire section of the contract that covers what warranties you will get for both the work done by the subs and the materials used. You want to find out what warranties the GC himself will provide on his subs' work, as well as on his own. Also, be sure that all manufacturers' warranties will be turned over to you.

Tip 40.19: Be sure there's a clause making the GC personally responsible for the job. Most GCs are doing business as corporations in order to insulate themselves from personal liability. If you can, however, you want his personal guarantee, because it is your best safeguard in case anything goes wrong.

Tip 40.20: The contract should require that the GC respond to the job supervisor as well as bring the supervisor in to check work whenever critically necessary. While some contractors might object to a mentor, that's too bad—price before pride.

Tip 40.21: How much supervision is required depends on the scope and complexity of what you're having done to your kitchen. A small job might require nothing more of the supervisor than a few trips to the job site to make sure the proper materials are being used and that work is proceeding apace. On the other hand, large, complex projects sometimes require daily supervision, including keeping tabs on both the GC and subs as well as the delivery of materials and fixtures.

Tip 40.22: Set ground rules in writing for the period of time when the GC, subs, and crews are in your home. For you, it's like the houseguests who came to stay. These individuals will be in and out of your house daily for a period of months, keeping their lunches in your refrigerator. Make it clear you want to be out of their way so they can work unimpeded. Guidelines should cover use of bathrooms, phone, and any other room that is not part of the kitchen renovation project.

41

Supplement your contract with detailed information. Your contract should also contain at least three supplements: a complete description of the project, including a list of all materials to be used and an explanation of all work to be performed; a listing of the charges for extras added to the plan prior to beginning work, and for changes made to the plan once the project has started, including what happens if the GC runs into surprises (like termites in the wall); and a list of the names and addresses of the companies (or individuals) who will honor manufacturer's warranties. The first two supplements will probably take the form of your finalized plans and specifications and the GC's finalized and accepted bid package.

☐ **Done**

42 Negotiate the terms of the agreement.

Irrespective of whether the contract originated with you or the contractor, the specific terms and language of the document must be negotiated.

☐ **Done**

Warning 42.1: Be prepared for the GC to push for as much money as he can get up front. Don't cave: if you're dealing with a sane, rational individual (and let's hope you are), who has decent credit (which you should already have checked) you should be able to limit the down payment to no more than 10 percent of the total price.

Warning 42.2: Most GCs like to add what's known as a force majeure or act of God clause to their contracts. This gives them additional time to complete a project if unforeseen circumstances—such as hurricanes, strikes, or labor shortages—occur. Make sure this clause is carefully worded to allow extra time for true acts of God, not for delays brought on by the contractor himself. However, the GC should bear the cost of finding replacements for any problems, even out-of-the-ordinary ones, that are foreseeable.

43 **Understand your rights to cancel.** After signing a contract for a remodeling project, in many states you may cancel the contract by midnight of the third business day after the signed transaction. The same holds true for contracts that will be paid in installments for more than ninety days. This three-day cancellation policy is generally not allowable in instances of emergency repair.

☐ **Done**

Tip 43.1: GCs are required by law to inform you of your cancellation rights and to provide you with a notice of cancellation form.

Tip 43.2: If for some reason you do want to cancel your contract within the allotted three-day period, be sure you send your cancellation notice by certified mail, return receipt requested.

DEALING WITH PROBLEMS DURING AND AFTER THE JOB

Kitchen renovations are guaranteed to have problems or at least complications for two reasons. First, kitchens are the most emotionally charged rooms in any home whether you cook often, once a year for the holidays, or not at all, and whether your family sits down together every night, only for Sunday brunch, or once a week for take-out Chinese. The kitchen is always the hearth of the home. Second, kitchens are the most complex rooms in any home since they involve every building system and sophisticated pieces of equipment. But just because problems are guaranteed to occur doesn't mean they can't be mitigated or dealt with.

44

Go with the flow. This means accepting the inevitability of something screwing up somewhere along the line, and being prepared to go with it, whatever it is. The screwup could be something as inane as the GC getting the flu, which could knock the renovation off schedule for a few days, or something more significant, like an unexpected rotten beam that needs replacing. It could also be you changing your mind and realizing that you really do want a bay window over the sink. But remember, part of what you pay the architect, construction manager, or designer for is to supervise and help smooth things along.

☐ **Done**

45

Mitigate problems through planning and communication. If possible, gather together everyone who will be working on your home, from the GC to the plumber, to discuss the project, individual schedules, etc. This can go a long way toward ensuring that things don't run overtime or over budget.

☐ **Done**

Tip 45.1: It is not uncommon for materials to be delivered late, thus holding things up. If you've got the room, have the GC order materials well ahead of time and then store them, making sure to check them carefully when they arrive. This is especially important for cabinets, which can take ten to twelve weeks to be delivered.

Tip 45.2: If, God forbid, there are any changes to the plans after work has already commenced, make sure all craftsmen involved in the job are aware of it.

Tip 45.3: The biggest obstacles you potentially face are surprises. Even the most careful planning cannot account for what is behind the walls— pest problems, wood rot, and metal stress will mean delays. Before any work begins, come to an agreement with the GC about how he'll handle these unanticipated obstacles.

Tip 45.4: If you have questions about what is going on during the course of the renovation, ask the GC. That includes specific questions you might have for a craftsman. The GC will be able to tell you when the best time might be to talk to one of the subs.

Tip 45.5: Should you change your mind about something that has already been completed, talk to the GC and request a change order. The GC will then figure out the cost of the change and submit it to you in writing. The order should be signed by both of you.

Warning 45.6: The GC or subs may try to substitute materials at the last minute. They will claim the substitution is necessary to prevent a long delay, although they may have other reasons for making the switch, like fatter profits.

Tip 45.7: The only way to guarantee that certain brands are used is to specify them in the contract. However, beware that even when brands are specified, if the contractor uses an alternate brand, it will be difficult to challenge him unless the alternate brand is *clearly* of inferior quality.

Warning 45.8: Don't let the GC or subs second-guess the kitchen designer. No changes in placement of appliances, center island, fixtures, etc., should be made without prior approval.

46 Watch your own behavior.

Your natural response to waste or delays might be to lash out at the construction crew who have invaded your home. Don't do it. Think how you'd feel if your boss had a conniption over your taking a coffee break at some point during your day. You'd be pretty annoyed, right? Well, that's exactly how the crew will feel if you turn into a harpy at the sight of them eating their lunch or taking a brief break. Anyway, you have a budget.

☐ **Done**

Tip 46.1: Be prepared for how a kitchen renovation project typically flows. Understand that, generally speaking, the first third of any job moves quickly, as demolition takes very little time. But then things seem to slow down. Finished work takes time, in addition to costing the most. So you'll feel as if the money being spent is out of proportion to the amount of progress on the job. And the slower the going, the more apt your blood pressure is to rise. But that's a perception only, not reality—let the professionals do their job and as long as inspection always precedes payment, you should not worry.

Warning 46.2: Keep out of the crafts-people's way. There's nothing wrong with putting in an appearance and asking a few questions. After all, this is your kitchen they're working on and your money they're spending. But you're not their apprentice, and if you follow them around making a nuisance of yourself, their annoyance will be reflected in their work.

Tip 46.3: Make the times of your visits to the kitchen to check out what's going on unpredictable. That will keep the crew on their toes.

Warning 46.4: When you do pay a visit, however, do not do your impression of the Inspector General. Should you spot anything that troubles you, make a mental note of it, then run it by the contractor. Remember: what seems like trouble or a mistake to your untrained and unprofessional eye could be one step in a process you don't understand.

Tip 46.5: Offering refreshments now and then is a good way to ingratiate yourself with the crew. They may be inclined to repay the favor with a favor of their own.

47 **Keep a list of any bona fide problems or mistakes—this will become your final punch list.** A punch list includes all the items that you and the architect discover when you make a final inspection. These need to be remedied by the GC or one of the subs. Make it clear to the GC that you won't consider the job done or hand over the money until the problems on the list are addressed.

☐ **Done**

48

Don't expect the inspector to be your supervisor. Don't be surprised if the visit by the building inspector is perfunctory. In most cases, the inspector will know the GC and the subs, and if she knows their past work has been up to snuff, the visit may be a mere formality.

☐ **Done**

Warning 48.1: Don't chide the building inspector if she isn't punctual. Putting in your two cents could turn a ten-minute once-over into a day-long examination and reveal violations that require considerable time and money to remedy. Resist the urge to talk about how your tax dollars go to her salary. Just bite your tongue and smile.

Warning 48.2: *Do not* bypass the building department and have the work done without obtaining the necessary permits. Yes, filing with the building department can cause delays and ultimately boost your real estate taxes, but working without a permit is illegal. Not only that, but building codes exist to make sure the work is done

properly and your home is safe. Work done on the sly will come back to haunt you. What happens when it comes time to sell your home, and the attorneys for the buyers find out you renovated your kitchen illegally and that the certificate of occupancy is invalid? If you ever need to make an insurance claim for damage to property, your insurer

can refuse to pay— and cancel your policy—if it discovers your certificate of occupancy isn't up to date.

49 Get advice on whether delays and overruns are understandable. You don't have to swallow every cost overrun or delay, even if it was caused by something as uncontrollable as a freak hailstorm. Since your GC knows what normal weather conditions are and what problems might surface, he should have taken them into account when preparing his bid and schedule. Try enlisting the help of your supervisory professional in these situations, asking her whether or not a particular problem or delay should have been foreseen.

☐ **Done**

50 Think carefully about how you'll resolve problems.

When a problem arises during your kitchen renovation you've got a decision to make. You can duke it out with your GC over who should foot the bill or eat the cost and pay it yourself, thus destroying your budget.

☐ **Done**

Tip 50.1: My advice? Seek the middle ground on problems that come up during the project. Suggest splitting the cost overruns, or offer to extend the completion date if you are asking the GC to bear the added cost. You want to avoid angering and/or potentially bankrupting the GC working on your house. Compromise if you can.

51

Make sure to get information from the GC that could be useful in the future. Before the GC leaves your house for the last time ask him for:

• the names and addresses of all the subs
• the names and addresses of all the manufacturers of all the materials and appliances
• any instruction booklets for the equipment

☐ **Done**

52

Be prepared for problems to arise after the job is finished. No matter how expert your craftsmen, the fact of the matter is your house is bound to settle, shift, expand, or contract, and there will be some glitches as a result. In fact, problems may come up six months to a year after the work is completed that are not covered by any specific warranty. The really good contractor will attend to them and that is why your choice in the beginning is so important.

☐ **Done**

Warning 52.1: Don't be surprised if you and your GC have differences of opinion over who is responsible for these after-completion problems. The GC may claim a problem is the manufacturer's responsibility or may be reluctant to return to your home, having lined up subsequent work. Don't back down: you're still holding the purse strings, and that gives you a tremendous amount of leverage. In addition, you've got the law on your side.

Tip 52.2: Call in your supervisory professional and have her mediate the problem if you feel you're not getting satisfaction. If she can't handle the matter, take it to the authority who licensed the contractor. This group has a lot of leverage with GCs, since they can review and possibly revoke his license.

Tip 52.3: In the unlikely event that the problem remains unresolved, bring the matter to the American Arbitration Association. This group has offices in most cities and can usually schedule hearings within a month. The "loser" must pay the association a fee of $150 and a percentage of the settlement. If your GC has

become financially insolvent in the interim, contact your area's consumer protection agency. Many have a small refund account for wronged consumers and may be able to give you at least a portion of the money the GC can't.

53 **Enjoy the fruits of your hard work.** With all the work done and the final glitches repaired, head into your beautiful new kitchen and fix a celebratory cup of cappuccino. While it may have cost you a little bit more money than if you had done it yourself, you should feel comforted by the fact that you did it *right*, using experts and avoiding numerous potential disasters. More important, you've made an investment that turned a house into a home.

☐ **Done**

GLOSSARY

APR or annual percentage rate: The cost of a loan expressed as a simple annual percentage, making it possible to compare various offerings.

architect: An individual educated and trained in the design of buildings; may be licensed or unlicensed, but should be a member of the American Institute of Architects (AIA).

construction manager: An individual educated, trained, and/or experienced in the management of construction projects and sites; often educated as a civil engineer or a former general contractor.

equity borrowing: A loan secured by the equity you have built up in your home; can take the form of either a straight home equity loan or a home equity line of credit accessed through a checkbook or credit card.

face-lifts: Kitchen renovations that focus on the exterior appearances of the room and its equipment; usually involving new appliances, fixtures, wall and floor coverings, countertops, and/or cabinet faces.

general contractor or GC: The chief of the crew of laborers and skilled workers who will be working on your project, responsible for the overall management and synchronization of the various tradesmen and craftsmen; sometimes also serves as one of the craftsmen, usually the carpenter.

hearth: Specifically the area in front of a fireplace, but most often taken to mean the symbol of domestic comfort and familial togetherness.

installment loan: An unsecured loan repaid in equal amounts over a predetermined period of time; if used specifically for a renovation, it's called a home improvement loan.

installment milestones: Discrete steps in a renovation project that are linked to specific payments.

interior designer: An individual educated and trained in the design of building interiors; should be a member of the American Society of Interior Designers (ASID).

kitchen planner: An individual educated and trained specifically in kitchen renovations; should be a Certified Kitchen Designer (CKD).

mortgage refinancing: The retirement and subsequent reissuing of a mortgage on your home; usually done either to lower monthly payments or to obtain cash from equity that has been built up—known as "cashing out."

overimprovement: A renovation that either costs more than it adds to the value of the structure or pushes the home over the top of the area's value range.

plans and specifications: a set of documents prepared by a planning professional; may include plans (overhead views), elevations (ground-level views), sections (cross-sectional views), details (sketches of ornamental or structural elements), and specifications (a list of features such as weights, colors, sizes, brand names, and model numbers).

punch list: A list of corrections, revisions, and repairs that need to be done before a renovation project can be considered complete.

remodeler: An individual educated and trained specifically in remodeling work; should be a Certified Graduate Remodeler (CGR) or a Certified Remodeler (CR).

remodeling: Altering the floor plan of a kitchen to increase the room's efficiency.

space additions: Adding on to the usable space in the kitchen; usually involves the addition of an informal dining or sitting area.

subcontractor or sub: An individual tradesman or craftsman, responsible for one element of the renovation project, answering to the general contractor; examples include electricians, plumbers, carpenters, masons, and roofers.

system upgrades: Improvements to the functional quality of the kitchen through the replacement of doors and windows, or electrical, plumbing, heating, or cooling systems.

teaser rate: An initially low rate of interest, used to attract borrowers, which is subsequently replaced by a higher rate of interest.

Printed in the United States
by Baker & Taylor Publisher Services